Stuff Every

# BIRD LOVER

Should Know

ALICE SUN

**QUIRK BOOKS**
PHILADELPHIA

Library of Congress Control Number: 2025940733

ISBN: 978-1-68369-514-1

Printed in China

Typeset in Figtree and Adobe Garamond Pro

Designed by Elissa Flanigan
Interior illustrations by Lucy Engelman
Cover illustrations by Olga Korneeva/Shutterstock.com
Production management by Mandy Sampson

Quirk Books
215 Church Street
Philadelphia, PA 19106
quirkbooks.com

MIX
Paper | Supporting
responsible forestry
FSC® C012521

Quirk Books' authorized representative in the EU for product safety and compliance is Easy Access System Europe, Mustamäe tee 50, 10621 Tallinn, Estonia, gpsr.requests@easproject.com.

10 9 8 7 6 5 4 3 2 1

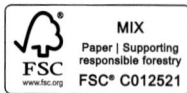

To those who stay curious

## BIRD-WATCHING AND BEYOND

## BRINGING BIRDS TO YOU

## FURTHER RESOURCES

# Introduction

*"Birds will give you a window, if you allow them."*
—Lyanda Lynn Haupt,
*Rare Encounters with Ordinary Birds*

If you're reading this book, you've most likely caught the bird-watching bug. Maybe it was a childhood interest that turned into a full-fledged passion. Or maybe you became enamored with our feathered friends more recently—when you sought out the slower paces of nature to cope with the pressures of modern life. Regardless, welcome. And congratulations: You're a bird person now.

It's a great time to get into birds. Technology has made it easier than ever to learn about and identify birds. Bird-watching has also become more diverse in recent years. LGBTQ+ folks, people of color, and those with mobility impairments have started their own birding groups to suit the needs of their communities, redefining what bird-watching is and who it's for. Birding is no longer just about chasing the most exotic species possible, reserved only for those who have the time and luxury to travel to far-flung places. Instead, a bird person is simply someone who's curious about their avian neighbors, whether they observe them in city parks or the remote wilderness.

If you're a curious person, there's much to learn when it comes to birds. Each species is full of surprises and has its own quirks. Human history has long been entangled with that of our feathered friends, and the world is full of stories of people daring to wonder what birds are and what they're capable of. In this book, I hope to not only touch on the basics of bird biology and bird-watching tips, but also give you the tools to dig into the weird and wonderful world of birds, from behavior to migration patterns to myths, folklore, and legend.

This book is pocket-sized for your convenience. Because the best thing about being a bird-watcher, I think, is that you can do it whether you're at home or on the go, no matter where you are in the world. Maybe you live in a more rural area and have flocks of snow geese visiting in the winter. Or maybe you're in a city, where pigeons, sparrows, and starlings have their own interesting interconnections with humanity. Regardless of where you are and how you got started, I hope this book gives you the answers you crave as well as a whole lot of new questions to explore on your own.

# BIRD BASICS

# What Makes a Bird?

Perhaps we as humans are so fascinated by birds because they're unlike any other creatures on earth, from their feathers to their hollow bones to the diversity of their nests and eggs and beaks. Most of all, their ability to fly has inspired the envy and the creativity of people for countless generations, culminating in the invention of the airplane in 1903. But to get a better understanding of what makes a bird, let's look into the deep past: the Mesozoic, or the age of dinosaurs.

## BIRDS ARE DINOSAURS

Birds are dinosaurs. Yes, you read that right. Although it may be hard to believe that your backyard chickadee is a relative of the T. rex, modern-day avians are in fact the closest thing we have to Jurassic Park in the world today.

Specifically, birds are the descendants of a very particular branch of dinosaurs called *theropods*—a family that includes the T. rex! These dinosaurs were bipedal and primarily carnivorous. They were also—unlike many mainstream dinosaur depictions—covered in sheaths of colorful feathers. Thanks to feathered fossils discovered in China over the past three decades, these dinosaurs have been reimagined by scientists and artists in recent years.

Toward the end of the Cretaceous Period, the final era of dinosaurs, many birdlike reptiles and early bird relatives flourished—until the fateful asteroid strike around 66 million years ago. Many of these dinosaurs perished in the mass extinction that followed, but curiously, some of them survived. How these feathered ancestors persisted is a subject of debate. Perhaps their protobeaks were better adapted to eating a wider variety of foods. Maybe it was just pure luck. Regardless, it was these survivors that eventually evolved into modern birds.

## THE FIRST BIRD

Paleontologists generally accept that the earliest true bird is *Archaeopteryx lithographica*. It lived in the late Jurassic Period around 150 million years ago, and the first fossil of this species was found in limestone deposits in Germany in the nineteenth century.

Upon examination, *Archaeopteryx* had a number of birdlike traits that led to this conclusion. For instance, it had wings and feathers along its arms. But *Archaeopteryx* also had distinct dinosaur features, like a bony tail. This is what makes it a transition fossil—a fossil that provides a missing evolutionary link between modern animals and their ancestors.

A number of other birdlike dinosaurs have been discovered in recent decades in the rocky deposits of China, like *Caudipteryx* and *Baminornis*, as well as some similar discoveries in North and South America. These fossils further support the theory that modern birds are descendants of dinosaurs.

This is what scientists think *Archaeopteryx*, the "first bird," may have looked like.

## BIRD EVOLUTION

Birds evolved a number of adaptations over the course of millions of years to make them, well, birds. These traits include:

**Hollow bones:** Bones with air sacs evolved to allow early birds to be lighter and more agile and have better oxygen circulation.

**Feathers:** These tubular structures likely started as an adaptation for insulation, but later evolved for flight and other functions.

**Fused bones:** Early birds evolved fused bones in the hands and feet, pelvis, tail, and collarbones (making the wishbone). This strengthened the skeleton for flight.

**Toothless bill:** Bird beaks don't have teeth, an adaptation that makes birds' skeletons lighter and more suitable for flight. Beaks have diversified in shape and size so that birds can consume different food types.

# Bird Families

How to sort animals into various related groups is a big question that taxonomists—scientists that specialize in the classification of organisms—set out to answer. The goal of taxonomy is not only to sort animals into groups, but also to do it in a way that accurately reflects evolutionary history.

A species is a taxonomic group that most everyone is familiar with. It's the smallest and most basic unit of categorization (although subspecies do exist). But animals are not just part of a species; they can also belong to a genus, family, order, or class, with class being the broadest category of the bunch. For instance, all birds belong to the class Aves, one of the larger categorizations in biological taxonomy.

The most useful levels of taxonomy to know, and perhaps the ones that best capture the diversity of birds, are orders and families. There are over ten thousand species of birds around the world that belong to over two hundred families, each having unique traits and adaptations. These groupings are constantly debated and shuffled as scientists make new discoveries about avian evolution and relationships.

Another thing to note about taxonomic groupings: They're not always organized by similar physical traits.

Long necks and legs are present in a number of birds, such as cranes and herons, but they are not all closely related. And falcons, which are small birds of prey, may look like hawks, but they are actually more closely related to parrots.

Knowing these subtleties can be frustrating at first (why didn't scientists pick easy traits like color to group birds?), but learning them is helpful as you dive deeper into the avian world, as they can help you navigate field guides and understand what various birds do and don't have in common.

## SOME BIRD GROUPS TO KNOW

To make matters more confusing, birders and bird scientists (called ornithologists) don't always use the same terminology. Some of the groups below are taxonomically accurate. Others have a more functional or intuitive reason to be lumped together. All are some common groupings that you may encounter in your bird-watching journey.

**Ratites:** The oldest extant birds in the world, ratites are flightless birds. This group includes ostriches, emus, cassowaries, tinamous, and more. They're probably the most dinosaur-looking birds out there.

Songbirds

Waterfowl

Ratites

Shorebirds

Raptors

Wading birds

Landfowl

They cannot fly because they lack a keel (a ridged breastbone), which makes them different from other birds. They are some of the largest birds in the world.

**Waterfowl:** The second oldest group of birds, waterfowl, is a group most are likely familiar with. Waterfowl include ducks, geese, and swans. If anyone has endured the wrath of a Canada goose (a.k.a. a hissing cobra chicken), they're likely acquainted with the dinosaur-like traits of these birds as well.

**Landfowl:** An order known as Galliformes, landfowl are your chickens, turkeys, quails, grouse, pheasants, peacocks, etc. Not exactly the smartest of the birds, landfowl play important roles in human society as domestic and game species.

**Raptors:** Raptors are birds of prey. They have sharp talons and beaks that can tear into flesh. Eagles, hawks, falcons, vultures, and a number of other birds are considered raptors, although based on taxonomy, these groups are not closely related to one another (for example, vultures are more closely related to storks than to other raptors).

**Owls:** Although owls are technically raptors, they are actually not closely related to hawks or eagles, as they belong in the order Strigiformes. Owls have several intriguing traits: They have forward-facing eyes, asymmetrical ears, soft feathers that render them silent in flight, and the ability to rotate their necks up to 270 degrees.

**Shorebirds:** Shorebirds are generally small, characterized by their long, thin beaks and legs, helpful for wading and probing in the muddy waters of the shorelines they favor. Shorebirds are in the order Charadriiformes, which also contain terns and gulls.

**Wading birds:** Wading birds are large birds that are typically found on the shores of bodies of water, including herons, egrets, spoonbills, and more. They typically nest in colonies and have long beaks to spear fish.

**Seabirds:** This group contains any bird that spends the majority of its life out at sea, such as puffins, penguins, albatross, murres, and more. They typically nest in colonies on remote islands and spend their winters wandering the ocean waves.

**Songbirds:** This is the largest and most diverse bird group and the one that evolved most recently (so they usually appear at the end of field guides). The oldest songbird is the lyrebird, a skilled songster that lives in Australia. All songbirds have developed vocal cords, which allow them to sing complex tunes that they use to attract mates, warn others of danger, and mark their territory.

## A Bird's Life Cycle

Because their reptilian ancestors laid eggs, birds, too, use this delicate capsule as their vehicle of reproduction. (For the record, if you want a scientific answer to the age-old question of "What came first, the chicken or the egg?" the answer is the egg, as eggs existed long before chickens did.)

The life of a bird begins with the egg and undergoes a winding journey before it becomes a fully fledged adult (literally).

### 1. THE EGG

After two birds mate and an egg is fertilized, the egg goes through a series of steps in a female bird's body. It starts out as a yolk. Then, the egg whites get coated over top. The egg is then enveloped in a series of membranes. The shell forms last, along with the pigments on it. The whole process takes around twenty-four hours. The female will lay her egg or eggs sometime in spring or summer (some birds, like great horned owls, will even lay their eggs in late winter).

### 2. INCUBATION

For weeks or months, one or both parents will take turns incubating their unhatched young beneath their feathers, keeping the egg at a toasty 98.6 degrees Fahrenheit. Spurred by the warmth, the embryo will undergo a dramatic transformation within the egg, developing the body parts it needs to survive.

### 3. HATCHING

When a chick is ready to hatch, it will start pecking at its shell using a special protrusion on its beak called the egg tooth. The chick will eventually poke a first small, then larger hole in the eggshell, from which it will slowly emerge. The egg tooth will dry and fall off around twelve to twenty-four hours after hatching.

### 4. THE CHICK

Depending on the species, there are two ways that a bird can spend the first few months of its life. If a species is *precocial*, like ducks or quails, the chick is ready to run around within hours of hatching. It will spend its young life trailing after its parent, oftentimes eating solid food on its own.

However, if a hatchling is *altricial* (like most song-birds), it often does not have feathers, eyesight, or the ability to move in its first vulnerable moments. It will reside in the nest, waiting for parents or other adults to come feed it regurgitated food.

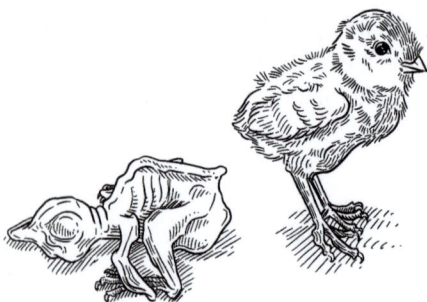

An altricial chick (*left*) and precocial chick (*right*)

## 5. FLEDGING

An important part of a young bird's life is reaching the fledgling stage, when they gain the ability to fly. As the chick grows, it will slowly molt its soft downy feathers and replace them with sturdier flight feathers. As these feathers grow, young birds will flap furiously, building their muscles and flying skills. The moment they leave the nest is their first step into independence.

## 6. MATURATION

After fledging, some birds will immediately reach sexual maturation the following spring, starting the cycle all over again. However, for a good number of birds it takes several years before they get to this stage.

For instance, bald eagles mature for four to five years before they get their characteristic white head. Gulls, too, will take several winters to reach full maturity.

What do they do during this time? It's no so different from human maturation. Crows, for example, which take three to four years to fully mature, will hang out with their families and other young birds, learning the ropes on how to be an adult crow before forming families of their own.

## Winging It: How Birds Fly

Birds are specially adapted for flight. In addition to (presumably) being fun as hell, flight allows birds to escape predators, access food sources in hard-to-reach places, and travel long distances to prime breeding grounds during migration (more on that later).

There are a few key traits that make birds the masters of flight:

- **Hollow bones** filled with air sacs make them lighter.
- **Toothless beaks**, instead of jaws, reduce weight.
- **Large breastbones** support the muscles that power the wings.
- **Streamlined bodies** are aerodynamic: Birds are usually torpedo shaped.
- **Wings** with lightweight feathers generate lift.

But how exactly do birds fly? To understand this, we have to get into a little bit of physics.

Because of the shape of their wings, birds are able to generate lift. This basically means that with each flap, the wind speed on the top of a bird's wing is greater than that on the bottom, reducing the air pressure up above. A flap can also direct air downward, further increasing lift.

To take off, birds push their legs off a branch, run across the ground, or paddle on the surface of the water to gain momentum. Once in the air, birds will adjust their wings and tail to guide their movement and direction. The tail acts like a rudder, directing the air flow, and birds generate forward motion by flapping their wings if they need to fly faster.

Some species or groups have a distinct way of flapping based on their anatomy and environment. For example, ducks flap vigorously because their bodies are quite heavy and their wings are on the smaller end, whereas albatrosses glide to preserve energy on their long journeys across the ocean. Hummingbirds flap mind-blowingly fast (up to seventy wingbeats per second) because they need to hover in place to feed on nectar.

## FLIGHTLESS BIRDS

Not all birds are able to take to the air. Scientists have long wondered if all flightless birds descended from the same ancestor, but genetic research in the early 2000s found that flightlessness actually evolved independently across multiple lineages. Distantly related flightless birds, like ostriches, penguins, and kiwis, all share similar traits: They have smaller wing bones and muscles than flighted birds. Flightless birds to tend to excel in other modes of transportation; for example, penguins are strong swimmers and ostriches excellent runners.

## BIRD RECORDS

**Fastest flying bird:** The peregrine falcon, which can reach top speeds of more than 200 mph (320 km/h)

**Heaviest flying bird:** The kori bustard, which at their heaviest can weigh more than 40 lb (18 kg)

**Fastest running bird:** The ostrich, which can reach top speeds of 43 mph (69 km/h)

**Largest bird:** Also the ostrich. Males can be up to 9 ft (2.8 m) in height and 290 lb (130 kg) in weight.

**Smallest bird:** The bee hummingbird, which only grows up to 2.2 in (5.5 cm) long and weighs less than 0.1 oz (about 2.6 g), around the size of an insect

**Largest wingspan:** The wandering albatross, which can have a wingspan of 11.5 ft (3.5 m)

## Light as a Feather

Feathers are remarkable adaptations. Only found in birds and their ancestors, feathers are made of the protein keratin, the same material as your fingernails. But unlike your fingernails, bird feathers are hollow and covered with interlocking plumes—and they come in a variety of forms. Fuzzy, downy feathers can keep a bird warm, whereas long swirly tail feathers can be used in mating displays. Despite their diversity, all feathers have the same general structure.

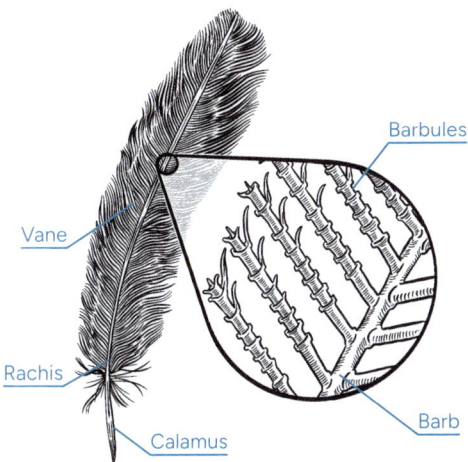

Barbules

Vane

Rachis

Calamus

Barb

The base of a feather is called the *calamus*, which extends into the *rachis*, the central vein of the feather. *Barbs* and smaller fibers called *barbules* then extend from the rachis, forming interlocking structures with one another. The result is a feather that not only is lightweight, but can be adapted for all sorts of functions.

## TYPES OF FEATHERS

**Wing:** Stiff, long feathers that are asymmetric and adapted for flight

**Tail:** Also known as rectrices, these feathers are long but symmetrical on both sides of the rachis and help a bird steer in flight.

**Contour:** Body feathers with fluffy bases, which are usually short and stout and provide some sort of waterproofing or protection

**Down:** Fluffy feathers that are close to a bird's skin, keeping them warm

**Semiplume:** Less fluffy than a down feather—the second layer of warmth

**Filoplume:** Rachis with a few barbs, which are used for sensing, like whiskers

**Bristle:** Just a rachis; usually found around the face to protect the eyes

## MOLTING

Birds replace their feathers throughout their life. Their first molt occurs when they lose their downy baby feathers and replace them with their first set of adult feathers (called their juvenile plumage). This process can take from a few days to up to a year. Some species have several juvenile molts since they take several years to mature.

Adult birds molt year after year, replacing their old feathers with fresh ones. Molting takes a lot of energy, so it typically occurs in late summer, between breeding and migration—two other energetically costly events in a bird's life. Small birds usually only molt once a year, whereas larger birds undergo this process twice.

Most birds molt their feathers bit by bit. Gulls, herons, and eagles molt their flight feathers in pairs—one on each wing—to maintain their ability to fly while avoiding imbalance (you may notice a gap in their wings in certain seasons). Ducks and geese are special cases: They undergo one molt a year, but they lose all their feathers at once. As a result, in the summer waterfowl are rendered mostly flightless—and they look very drab and disheveled in the process (this is called the eclipse plumage). This is why you'll see mallard males without their characteristic green heads in the summer.

Some birds will also alternate between summer and winter plumage. For instance, snow buntings have breeding plumage that is pure white with black wingtips. But in the winter, their plumage is mottled with beige and brown to help them camouflage. Similarly, American goldfinches are bright yellow in the spring and summer but look duller in the colder months.

# Decoding Beaks

Birds do not have teeth, so their beaks need to be specially adapted to process their meals and break down their food. Charles Darwin was one of the first biologists to note this. His famous Galápagos finches all had different beaks depending on the island that they lived on and the food that was available.

There are many types of bird beaks. Some are particularly noteworthy and adapted specifically to the bird's primary food source.

Clockwise from top left: carnivorous, fruit-eating, fish-scooping, filter-feeding, mud-probing

**Generalist:** Generalists like crows have a beak that's suited for any meal, from seeds to fruit to shellfish.

**Nectar-feeding:** Hummingbirds, honeycreepers, and sunbirds all have long bills that can get into flowers and reach the nectar that lies within.

**Insectivorous:** The small and stout beaks of insectivorous birds, such as swallows, swifts, and nightjars, help them snag moths and mosquitoes from midair.

**Seed-eating:** Seed-eating birds, like finches, sparrows, and grosbeaks, have cone-shaped bills that allow them to break through the hard shells of seeds.

**Fruit-eating:** Fruit-eating birds, like toucans and hornbills, have large, long beaks that are adapted to pick and smush fruits.

**Carnivorous:** The hooked bill of a raptor allows it to dig into feathers, fur, and flesh. The hooked bills of scavengers like vultures and condors usually lack feathers around them, to keep things clean when they dig into bones and rotting carcasses.

**Woodpecking:** The sharp bill of a woodpecker is the perfect chisel for smashing bark to get at the bugs beneath.

**Filter-feeding:** Filter-feeding bills, like those of flamingos and ducks, have fine sieves within that allow these birds to sift out water and leave invertebrates and/or vegetation behind.

**Mud-probing:** The long bills of shorebirds allow them to probe deep into the mud so that they can catch invertebrates underground.

**Fish-scooping:** The pouch-like beak of a pelican helps it scoop fish out of the water.

## GIZZARDS

In addition to a beak, birds also have "toothed" sacs in their throats called gizzards. These compartments squish and grind especially hard-to-digest foods like seeds. Sometimes birds will even swallow rocks to help facilitate this grinding process. When the rocks become too smooth, they will be regurgitated and replaced with newer, sharper stones.

# BIRD

# BEHAVIOR

# Birdsong

Birds do strange and fascinating things. As you observe the birds around you, you may wonder what purpose these behaviors serve. Many bird behaviors are linked to a bird's life cycle and survival, and birdsong is a great example of this.

In early spring, you might begin waking up to a cacophony of birdsong. The beginning of the day is when most birds sing, and this abundance of song is referred to as the dawn chorus. Although scientists aren't entirely sure why birds pick the wee hours of the morning to belt out their songs, it is a great time to listen to some of the avian world's best vocal talents—and to learn who sounds like what. Some birds will sing all day. Some will pick their songs back up at dusk.

Birdsong has a variety of functions, including defending breeding territory and attracting a mate. Songbirds, which have evolved complex vocal cords, tend to have the most beautiful and complex songs, which can take years to learn and perfect. Interestingly, some songbirds even have regional dialects in their music, since songs are passed down from one generation to the next. Next time you travel, notice if the songs of familiar birds sound just a little bit different.

## BIRD CALLS

Singing usually dies down sometime in midsummer, when most birds are nesting or raising chicks. But that doesn't mean that birds go completely quiet. Birds have calls as well as songs—usually shorter, less elaborate noises they make to communicate with other birds. Some calls, like the high-pitched *pik* of an American robin or the *dee-dee-dee* of a black-capped chickadee, are used to communicate alarm or the presence of a threat.

## FEMALE BIRDS SING TOO!

In recent years, ornithologists have discovered that it's not just male birds that sing during the breeding season. More than 70 percent of songbird species have females that sing; most of these species live in the tropics. Researchers think that females sing for similar reasons as males do: to defend territories and attract mates. And who's to say that they don't also sing for the sheer joy of it?

# Mating

Once a bird attracts a mate, then the real show begins. With their hormones raging, birds engage in elaborate displays to really impress their potential partner, in which they show off their best physical aspects and their ability to be a caring mate. For example, red-capped manakins will moonwalk, blue-footed boobies will show off their colorful feet, and mourning doves will preen and feed each other. Here are a few more examples of mating behaviors.

**Synchronized dances:** Western grebes gather in the freshwater lakes of the American West every spring. Once they have found a potential mate, the pair will engage in a dance, mirroring each other. The dance's final pinnacle is when the two launch themselves out of the water, necks outstretched, feet pedaling, hovering across the water as a duo.

**Dance battles:** The greater sage-grouse, like many grouses, will engage in what are called leks. These are essentially dance battles, in which males will gather in an open spot in the sagebrush desert and dance their butts off. First they puff up their plumage and fan out their tails. They then inflate their bizarre-looking throat pouches, holding their wings close along their body to make a swishing sound as they pop their air sacs with a *pop-whistle-pop* that echoes in the morning air.

**Death-defying drops:** Bald eagle pairs, like many raptors, will engage in a precarious aerial display. The two birds will circle each other high in the sky, performing a series of dives. Then, the two birds will lock their talons—spiraling toward the ground and pulling apart only at the last minute.

**Bird houses:** Male house wrens need to have top-notch construction skills to attract a mate. If a female is in his area, he'll lead her to his nest cavity, where she'll conduct a thorough inspection. If the nook is up to her standards, she'll start constructing her nest within.

**Gifts:** Cedar waxwing pairs will hop toward each other, sometimes touching beaks. Males will sometimes pass along a small gift—a berry, insect, or flower petal—that the female will take, hop away with, and then return to the male. This repeats until the female eats the gift.

## HOW DO BIRDS MATE?

The reproductive anatomy of birds is very different from that of mammals. Both males and females have a cloaca, a single opening where feces, urine, eggs, and sperm all come out of (not at the same time!). This is a by-product of their reptilian ancestry. During breeding season, the cloaca is enlarged so the male can pass his sperm to the female to fertilize her egg, starting a bird's life cycle. The exchange is often referred to as a cloacal kiss.

## BIRD BREAKUPS

Most birds, an estimated 90 percent of them, are monogamous, meaning that they stay with the same mate during a breeding season—or even for life! However, that doesn't mean the love lives of birds aren't messy. Bird breakups can happen in the real world, and throuples—which scientists call extra-pair copulations—also exist. There are also some bird species that are polygamous (males have multiple partners) and polyandrous (females have multiple partners).

## GAY PENGUINS?

In the late nineties in New York City's Central Park Zoo, two male penguins, Roy and Silo, coupled together and dutifully took care of an egg when it was given to them. They hatched and raised the chick, Tango, sparking a media frenzy and inspiring a popular children's book, *And Tango Makes Three*. Yes, gay penguins are possible; nature is very queer!

A number of same-sex relationships in many types of birds have long been documented by scientists. Chilean flamingos, black swans, acorn woodpeckers, and countless other species have been observed in male homosexual relationships. Some have even successfully raised young, either via temporary trysts with females or by adopting a life of crime and stealing eggs. In some bird species, like the Laysan albatross, female birds will often pair up and raise chicks together.

## Nesting

Conglomerations of sticks, mud, feathers, plastic bottle caps, and anything in between, bird nests are marvelous structures. Each species—and individual bird—has a unique way of building them, and nests are influenced by the materials available. For example, magpies in Europe have been observed using bird spikes (meant to keep birds off of buildings) in their nests, a form of seeming rebellion against antibird architecture. Birds can also influence one another with their nests shapes, passing this cultural practice between generations.

At the fundamental level, nests are cradles for a bird's egg or chicks. Their primary function is to provide a safe place for a bird to keep their eggs and raise their young. Usually, but not always, nests are concealed or placed out of the reach of predators. As a result, bird nests can be found in a variety of locations—up high in trees, along cliffs, deep in the undergrowth, burrowed underground, or in a parking lot.

Some nests are more extravagant than others. Perhaps the most familiar is a mass of carefully placed sticks with eggs nestled in the center, like that of the American robin. But nests can also be woven sacks,

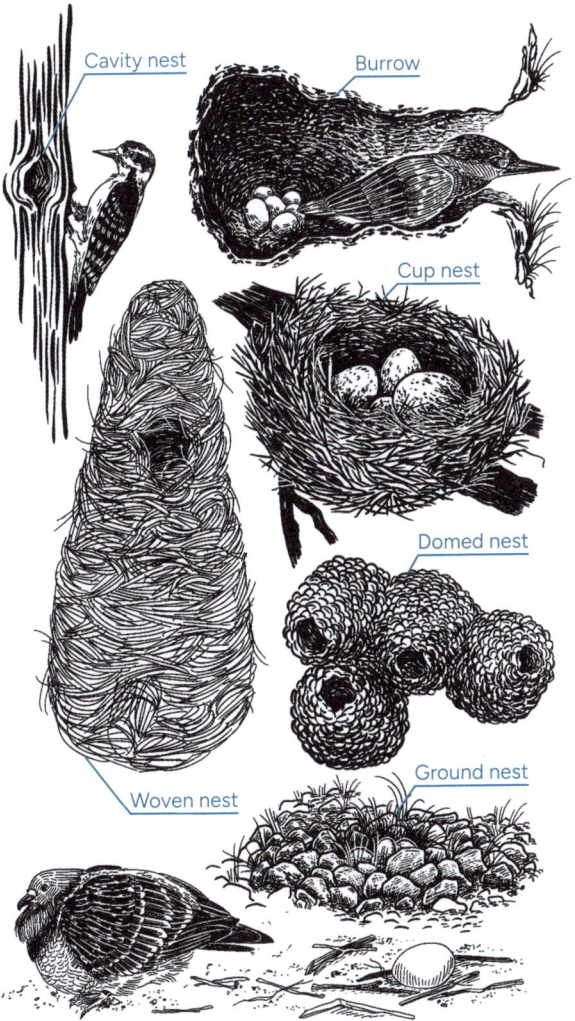

Cavity nest

Burrow

Cup nest

Domed nest

Ground nest

Woven nest

like those of orioles, who use grass to construct a sock-like tube. Cliff swallows, on the other hand, combine mud and their saliva to build shelters on the walls of cliffs or on ledges underneath bridges. Kingfishers will burrow tunnels into soft soil and lay their eggs within. Cavity-nesters, like prothonotary warblers, will use existing tree cavities made by woodpeckers as a place to raise their young. Others, like killdeer, will build a simple depression in rocky soil. Pigeons are notoriously bad nest makers, sometimes laying eggs on bare ground (but they get by anyway).

## EGGS

Just like nests, bird eggs are also beautiful and diverse. They come in a variety of different colors and patterns. Colors can help eggs camouflage or help a bird recognize their own eggs.

Shapes of eggs also differ between bird species and are adapted for their corresponding lifestyles. For instance, scientists have found that cliff-nesting birds, like murres or guillemots, have long eggs that taper to a thin point at the top. This shape is thought to prevent the eggs from rolling off the cliff, although scientists have yet to find adequate evidence to support this idea.

## BROOD PARASITISM

Not all birds will make their own nests or raise their own young. Some birds are brood parasites, meaning that they will lay their eggs in the nests of other bird species. They'll sneak into the nest when the owner isn't around, leaving their young to be cared for by the unsuspecting host. In many cases, hosts will incubate and raise the foreign chick as their own, although some species have learned to detect and eject the young of such tricksters.

Cuckoos and brown-headed cowbirds are examples of brood parasites. They will usually parasitize small songbirds like warblers, who end up with chicks that are much bigger than they are!

### NESTS ARE *NOT* FOR SLEEPING

Outside of the breeding season, birds do not actually sleep in nests. They instead shelter in roosting spots—usually in a tree or, for aquatic birds, in a protected bay. Woodpeckers, adorably, will cling vertically to a tree to sleep.

Some birds roost alone, whereas others do so communally. For example, American crows can congregate in trees in the millions.

## Foraging

As the diversity of their beaks would suggest, birds eat a wide variety of foods—including (but not limited to) berries, seeds, nectar, invertebrates, small mammals, and, yes, even other birds! Birds can be categorized as one of the following types of feeders:

- **Hunters:** birds that wait for and then pounce on their prey
- **Foragers:** seed- or fruit-eating birds that travel from food source to food source
- **Opportunists:** birds that eat a wide variety of foods and will adapt their behavior according to what's available

But like all categories in nature, the boundaries between these three groups are messy. Bald eagles are hunters, but can also be opportunistic and have been observed feasting in landfills. Buffleheads are piscivorous (fish-eating) diving ducks, but will occasionally eat grains. Some birds are specialists and have behaviors that don't fall into any of these categories, such as nectar-sipping honeycreepers.

Birds can also be categorized by the specific foods they eat, including:

- **Granivorous:** seed-eating
- **Frugivorous:** fruit-eating
- **Piscivorous:** fish-eating
- **Insectivorous:** insect-eating
- **Carnivorous:** meat-eating
- **Omnivorous:** having a flexible diet

## FEEDING TIME

Not all birds feed during the day. Nocturnal birds, such as most owls and nightjars, feed mainly under the cover of darkness. Birds that feed during the day are referred to as diurnal, whereas birds that are most active during dawn and dusk are crepuscular.

## INTERESTING FEEDING BEHAVIORS TO LOOK FOR

Keep an eye out for feeding behaviors as you observe the birds around you. These behaviors, in addition to the birds' appearance and calls, can be helpful in the identification process.

**Diving:** To catch fish or other seafood delicacies, cormorants, diving ducks, and other seabirds will plunge underwater. Under the surface, they'll flap their wings in pursuit of their prey. Notably, northern gannets will hover high in the sky before nose-diving straight into the water. Emperor penguins have been observed diving to depths of 1,800 feet and staying underwater for up to twenty-three minutes in search of food.

**Filter feeding:** Watch dabbling ducks slurp up pond water in search of aquatic plants and invertebrates. Flamingos are also filter feeders, but with a twist. Because of their unique bills, they filter water upside down, gorging on small red shrimp (which give their feathers their characteristic pink color).

**Poking and prodding:** Shorebirds continually poke at the mud with their long bills while feeding. Within this feeding group, each species has its own characteristic foraging rhythm. Yellowlegs are elegant, sweeping along the water in a zigzag motion. Sandpipers are busy and energetic, running and prodding nonstop. Plovers will run, pause, and then pounce. Learning feeding behaviors is especially helpful for shorebird identification.

**Attacking from above:** Hunters like hawks, eagles, kingfishers, or herons often wait in one place, watching for their prey. When a meal gets within range, they strike, snagging their prey in their beaks or talons. However, the success rate of hunters is low, and often they'll come up empty.

**Erratic flying:** Insectivores like swallows, swifts, and nighthawks will fly in erratic patterns in the sky, twisting and turning so that they can catch insects, such as moths, in midair. Many insectivores are crepuscular, feeding at dawn and dusk when moths and other insects are most active.

**Tree gleaning:** *Gleaning* refers to a style of feeding in which birds collect insects from trees and foliage. You might spot small warblers, vireos, and kinglets doing this in the treetops. They rarely stop moving, jumping from branch to branch in search of caterpillars hidden amongst the leaves.

**Tree scaling:** Nuthatches, black-and-white warblers, and brown creepers are small birds that crawl up (or down) tree trunks. They do this because they specialize in eating bark-dwelling insects. Interestingly, brown creepers tend to climb a tree upward, whereas a nuthatch will climb downward.

**Tree drilling:** If you hear drumming in the forest, it's most likely a woodpecker at work. These birds will drive their beaks into a tree so they can get at the insects and larvae underneath the bark. Different species of woodpeckers will leave behind differently shaped holes. For example, pileated woodpeckers make large, squarish holes. Downy woodpeckers carve out a trail of smaller holes.

**Sap sipping:** A type of woodpecker, sapsuckers drill rows of holes on trees and will periodically return to sip up the sap that flows out.

**Nectar sipping:** Hummingbirds travel from flower to flower and hover in place while they sip up nectar. They are aggressively territorial and will guard their flower patch or hummingbird feeder with fervor.

**Ground scratching:** Ground foragers like sparrows, juncos, and towhees will scratch at the ground, moving leaf litter aside so that they can find any seeds or invertebrates hiding underneath.

# Bird Brains: Cognition and Intelligence

Although the term *bird-brained* is typically reserved for someone with subpar intelligence, birds, as a whole, are actually quite smart. Notably, parrots and corvids (a group of birds containing crows, ravens, and jays) have long been a subject of fascination for those who study animal cognition and intelligence. These two groups have relatively large brains in proportion to their body sizes, and their brains are packed with neurons—twice the amount as in a primate brain of around the same size. In contrast, chickens and ostriches have the smallest brain-to-body-size ratio and are considered less intelligent in the bird world.

Over the years, scientists have documented many types of birds accomplishing impressive feats of cognition. Here is just a small selection:

## TOOL-USING AND TOOL-MAKING

Many birds have been documented using tools, a complex behavior also seen in orangutans and chimps. Green herons will toss a stick or leaf into the water to attract fish. American crows will drop mussels onto concrete to crack them open. Woodpecker finches will use sticks to grab insects from crevices. Notably, the

New Caledonian crow, considered one of the smartest birds in the world, is able to make compound tools, joining two objects together to form a hook that it uses to snag a meal with.

## MEMORIZATION

Chickadees have fantastic memories and are able to recall every single location where they've hidden food—which can be up to five thousand stashes a day. They also wipe their memories every year, annually repopulating their brains with new memories of food caches during the colder months.

## FACIAL RECOGNITION

In an experiment at the University of Washington, which began in 2006, scientists discovered that crows can remember faces. For the study, the lead researcher wore a caveman mask while he caught crows and banded them (a research method in which scientists put numbered metal bands on birds' legs so that they can be identified later). The crows remembered the mask and the traumatic experience of being caught and shared this information with their family members. For nine years after, the crows would mob this researcher whenever he wore the mask.

## GIFTING

The same University of Washington scientist has noted another curious behavior in crows: They'll bring trinkets to the people who feed them. He's heard many anecdotes of people who feed their backyard corvids in exchange for rocks, buttons, coins, bottle caps, jewelry, acorns, and more. A number of similar encounters have gone viral on the internet. This behavior isn't well studied, but scientists aren't surprised that crows engage in this type of gift-giving.

## SONG-LEARNING

Birds learn how to sing songs from other birds (as noted in "Birdsong" on page 36). The ability to do this is called vocal learning, and it functions similarly to how we learn language as children: by copying, interpreting, practicing, and experimenting. Young birds have a period in their lives when they sing various random noises, called *sub-song*. This is much like when a human baby babbles.

## MIMICRY AND LANGUAGE-LEARNING

Mockingbirds are notorious mimics. They can learn up to two hundred songs drawn from the sounds around them, from creaky gates to car alarms. Parrots—most notably Alex the African gray parrot, the famous subject of a thirty-year-long study by animal psychologist Irene Pepperberg—have been documented as having a working vocabulary up to one hundred human words. This is the equivalent of a human two-year-old's vocabulary.

## PLAYING

Ravens, like a number of other corvids, are known to be very social. Although they will often fight with one another to establish social hierarchy, they will also play, it seems, just for the fun of it. Bird-watchers have observed them rolling around in the snow and tossing pancake-shaped snowballs, "tobogganing" down roofs on plastic lids, and teasing domestic animals like cats and dogs.

# Flocking Together

Many birds form flocks. Starlings are the most famous example, forming stunning murmurations and patterns in the sky. Ducks and geese also come together in large numbers in the winter—think of a honking flock of Canadian geese passing overhead. Shorebirds form giant groups during migration.

So why do birds do this? Flocks can benefit birds in the following ways:

**Predator protection:** A big benefit of flocking is safety in numbers. A group of birds is much better at spotting predators than a lone bird is. It's harder for predators to single out a target when multiple birds are present. A flock can also fight back, mobbing a predator and pushing it out of the area.

**Information sharing:** Coming together can help birds learn from other birds. They can follow each other to food sources or guide one another along the best migration path. Research has shown that starlings switch direction based on the cues of the seven closest birds around them, enabling them to respond to a threat without even seeing it.

**Energy saving:** Some species, like geese, fly in special V formations. This is because, with each flap, a bird is generating wind that the one behind it can surf on, helping them save energy while undergoing long journeys.

**Nest safety:** Some birds exclusively breed in dense colonies, in which nests of different families are built right next to one another. Having so many nests together is helpful because parents can depend on their neighbors to protect their young as well.

**Warmth:** Huddling up with the flock, especially in the winter or on cold nights—as penguins famously do—can be a way for birds to keep warm.

## COLLECTIVE NOUNS FOR BIRDS

Most of us have heard of a brood of hens or a flock of geese, but the world of birds is full of fascinating collective nouns. These terms sometimes communicate something about the personality or behaviors of these birds.

- A murmuration of starlings
- A murder of crows

- A gaggle of geese
- A commotion of coots
- A parliament of owls
- A flamboyance of flamingos
- A bevy of quails
- A kettle of hawks
- A raft of ducks
- A charm of finches
- A cloud of blackbirds
- A cote of doves
- A confusion of guinea fowl
- A pouch of pelicans
- A bouquet of pheasants
- A conspiracy of ravens
- A mischief of magpies
- A pandemonium of parrots

## FLOCK BEHAVIORS

*Mobbing* is when birds come together in large groups to attack or intimidate a threat, often a larger, predatory bird like a raptor. *Murmurations* are large groups of birds that form mesmerizing patterns with their movements. It's usually used to refer to starlings, but other birds can also form these large swirling flocks.

## MIXED-SPECIES FLOCKS

Not all flocks are exclusively made up of members of the same species. Birds of different feathers can flock together, too. Especially during migration, birds will travel in mixed-species flocks; for example, warblers, vireos, chickadees, flycatchers, and other songbirds will often stick together. Mixing with other species is advantageous. Every species has its own strengths and can keep an eye out for different predators and threats.

## FLYING SOLO

Perhaps surprisingly, not many birds are truly solitary. There are some exceptions: Roadrunners, most woodpeckers, some sandpipers, and rails all live a relatively secluded existence. But depending on the season, whether there's an abundant food source or other environmental factors, more solitary birds do come together. Birds of prey, such as hawks, migrate in groups; they gather in warm columns of rising air called thermals. Eagles, notably in the Pacific Northwest, gather in large numbers to take advantage of the annual salmon run. Herons, often lone fishers, also breed in colonies.

# Migration

One of the great marvels of the avian world is migration: the annual journey that birds make between their summer and winter homes. Over half of North American birds are migratory, meaning that billions of birds travel across the continent, and around the world, every year.

Most of these movements are driven by food and reproduction. Some birds breed in places like the Arctic because this area has relatively few predators but also abundant invertebrates and plant matter to snack on and feed their young. Migrants then leave these spots in the fall to spend their winters in warmer locales, like tropical rainforests or seaside mangroves.

However, not all migratory birds undertake grand journeys every year. There are a few different migration patterns to note:

**Long-distance migrants:** These are birds that travel across the world, usually between the tropics and the Arctic.

- Long-distance migrants include the long-billed curlew, Blackburnian warbler, and red knot.

**Medium-distance migrants:** These birds take on moderate journeys, around a few hundred miles.

- Medium-distance migrants include the blue jay and eastern bluebird.

**Short-distance migrants:** Some birds undergo shorter seasonal journeys, usually from higher elevations in the summer to lower elevations in the winter (called *altitudinal migration*). Short-distance migrants may also move from more forested habitats to fields to follow food sources.

- Short-distance migrants include the dark-eyed junco, northern saw-whet owl, and red-winged blackbird.

**Permanent residents:** Nonmigratory birds stay in one area year-round.

- Permanent residents include the northern cardinal and black-capped chickadee.

**Partial migrants:** A species is considered a partial migrant when some birds within the species migrate and some don't. In other words, some populations of partial migrants are permanent residents, whereas others will move in the spring and fall.

- Partial migrants include American robins and killdeer.

**Irruptive migrants:** Bird migration doesn't always follow seasonal patterns. Irruptive migrants, also called nomadic migrants, have highly variable movement patterns, tailoring their migrations to the rhythms of their food source.

- Irruptive migrants include the snowy owl, redpoll, and red-breasted nuthatch.

## MIGRATORY FLYWAYS

Long-distance migrants of the world follow tried and true pathways called migratory flyways. These migration superhighways are routes that are used by billions of birds every year, and the knowledge of these paths are passed down between generations.

Worldwide, there are ten migratory flyways: four in the Americas and six encompassing Eurasia, Africa, and Australasia.

## NOTABLE MIGRATIONS

**Longest migration:** The bird with the longest migration is the Arctic tern. These birds travel from the North Pole, where they breed, to the South Pole, where they winter, every year, traveling an average total of 25,000 miles per year. They are also known to eat and sleep while in the air and can spend months without touching the ground.

**Shortest migration:** The bird with the shortest migration is the dusky grouse (formerly known as the blue grouse). It travels as little as 1,000 feet (about 300 meters) between coniferous and deciduous forests in the Rocky Mountains.

**Longest nonstop migration:** Bar-tailed godwits undertake the longest nonstop migration, traveling between Alaska and New Zealand/Australia in a single flight.

**Fastest migration:** Whimbrels are one of the world's fastest migrants. They are able to reach speeds of up to 100 miles an hour by riding the winds of hurricanes and other air currents.

## HOW BIRDS NAVIGATE

Although it's not entirely understood how birds navigate during migration, there are a few main theories. Birds most likely use all of these cues in tandem to orient themselves on their journeys.

**The sun:** Research has shown that birds use their internal clocks, also called their circadian rhythm, to infer the position of the sun, which informs their direction. Experiments on starlings and pigeons have shown that if you manipulate the amount of light and dark a bird is experiencing, which messes with their circadian rhythm, their navigation system is also impaired.

**The stars:** In a famous experiment in the 1970s, an ornithologist at Cornell University put indigo buntings, which are nocturnal migrants, in a planetarium. He found that if he reversed the star pattern, the buntings also changed their direction.

**Magnetism:** The Earth has a magnetic field, generated by the planet's molten core. Scientists have long theorized that birds can sense this magnetic field, possibly through their beaks or inner ears. More recently, research published in 2022 has demonstrated that common reed warblers have special light-sensing proteins in their eyes that are triggered when there are changes in the Earth's magnetic field, meaning that they may be able to "see" the magnetic field and use its fluctuations to migrate.

**Landmarks:** Birds can remember landmarks, such as an island, a building, or even a particular tree. Homing pigeons are able to retrace their flight paths by memorizing the landscape.

**Smell:** Scent-sensitive seabirds like Scopoli's shearwaters use smell to navigate the vast oceans.

## HARK, A VAGRANT BIRD!

Birds can sometimes find themselves in unexpected locales outside of their usual range. These birds are called *vagrants* and can lose their way due to:

- **Bad weather:** Strong winds or other storms can force a bird to prematurely stop on their journey or can push them off course.
- **Inexperience:** Vagrants tend to be juvenile birds that are undertaking their first-ever migration in

the fall. They usually get lost because they are unfamiliar with the landscape and have taken a wrong turn.

- **Solar storms:** Solar storms can jettison particles that disrupt the magnetic field, potentially altering a bird's navigation system and steering it off course. Scientists have found that vagrancy often increases during the fall migration due to solar storms.

Often vagrants will move on, finding their way back to their flight path, but some decide to stick around and can even survive and thrive in unfamiliar territory. (See page 111 for tips on what to do when you spot a vagrant.)

# OUR

# FEATHERED

# FRIENDS

## Domestication

Birds are deeply intertwined with human history. Over millennia, birds have provided humans with key sources of food (poultry and eggs) and materials (including down feathers, guano, and more).

Throughout history, humans have domesticated numerous species of birds for these benefits. Domestication is a process wherein people tame animals, putting them under human care so that they can harness the animals for food, clothing, materials, and companionship. Over time, through selective breeding, these domesticated breeds adapt more and more closely to life with humans. So when did this close relationship with birds begin?

### GEESE

Anthropologists have discovered that the oldest confirmed domesticated bird is the goose—more specifically, the swan goose, also known as the Chinese goose. Scientists uncovered goose bones from seven thousand years ago in a small rice cultivation village near the lower Yangtze River in China. Egyptians were also domesticating geese more than four thousand years ago, and in ancient Greece, geese made appearances in stories like *The Odyssey*.

Today, as in the past, geese are a source of food, eggs, and down feathers. Some also keep these spirited birds as companions. In contrast to their wild cousins, some domesticated geese are pure white, a color that's characteristic of a number of domesticated fowl.

## CHICKENS

Chickens were domesticated around three thousand to five thousand years ago, when people in Southeast Asia unintentionally attracted the junglefowl to their harvests after they began cultivating rice. The birds then arrived in the Mediterranean roughly 2,800 years ago and later appeared in Africa around one thousand years ago.

Today, chicken is the most popular meat in the world. Globally, around 140 million metric tons of chicken is consumed per year. At any given moment 27.6 billion domestic chickens are alive, producing both meat and eggs—and outnumbering humans more than three to one. People have also kept chickens as pets or for sport. Cockfighting—pitting male chickens against each other in a duel—was a popular contest in ancient China, Greece, and Rome. It's still conducted for some religious purposes, but banned in most countries due to animal cruelty laws.

## TURKEYS

Around two thousand years ago, Mayans in Mesoamerica first domesticated turkeys. The large fowl caught the attention of early Spanish explorers. They plopped the birds on ships and took them home to Europe, where they became a popular farm bird and dish at the dinner table. It was here that they got their name—turkey—since Europeans confused the American bird with the guinea fowl that was commonly sold by the Turks.

When European colonists traveled to North America, they then brought these birds home to their original continent. As a result, North America is home to both domestic and wild turkeys, in a roundabout journey. By the early twentieth century, wild turkeys were nearly extinct in the United States due to overhunting and habitat loss. Their numbers have since recovered thanks to hunting regulations, habitat protection, and reintroduction efforts.

## PIGEONS

Relatively little is known about how pigeons came to be domesticated. The first written records of pigeons are from ancient Mesopotamia around five thousand years ago, although some scholars posit that domestication happened long before then. There have been other hints of our ancient relationship with pigeons, including Egyptian hieroglyphs that make mention of pigeons as a part of ritual sacrifices.

By the eighteenth century, Europeans had begun began to breed different types of pigeons. This artificial selection created a range of pigeons with different traits, including "fancy" pigeons—ones with beautiful colors and feathers that were kept as pets—and homing pigeons: birds that excel in navigation and speed, bred for racing and sending messages.

Over the years, some domesticated pigeons escaped their human keepers, allowing them to establish feral populations in cities, adapting to the skyscrapers that mimic the cliffs of their natural habitats. These are the pigeons that many of us are familiar with today. In many places, they're considered pests because of their abundant droppings, earning them the nickname "rats with wings," despite their former glory days.

# Pet Birds

Birds like parrots, parakeets, and finches make great pets because of their high intelligence, social tendencies, and ability to form bonds with humans. Although these pets are tame, they're not considered domesticated. That's because most pet birds are direct descendants of wild birds that were born in captivity. They haven't been bred over many generations to have domesticated traits, the way pigeons and geese have.

The pet trade, however, did begin thousands of years ago. Humans have long captured birds from their local areas and kept them as companions. People in Brazil kept parrots as pets. Ancient Romans took an affinity to parakeets. The British caged their goldfinches. As global navigation began to develop, people became fascinated by birds from faraway places. Parrots, due to their intelligence and mimicry, were in particular demand in Europe by the upper class after Christopher Columbus brought some back from his journey to the Americas.

As global trade developed, wild birds began to be exchanged around the world. Pheasants and parrots from India and South America were shipped to Europe to be part of menageries and zoos. Peacocks wandering one's lawn became a symbol of status.

African
gray parrot

Cockatiel

Zebra
finches

Lovebirds

Budgie

As Europeans colonized America, so did their pet birds. Working-class families had caged birds like cardinals and mockingbirds, whereas the wealthy had larger aviaries.

By the early twentieth century, many birds were nearing extinction, so laws were passed banning at-risk species and migratory birds from being kept in captivity in the United States. Those same laws did not apply to tropical birds, which is why so many of our pet birds today come from warmer locales. Many birds, too, like the painted bunting, are still illegally trapped and sold to the underground pet trade for profit.

## COMMON PET BIRDS

**Cockatiels** are friendly birds with lots of personality. They can learn to talk and sing and can live up to twenty years.

**Budgies** are very popular pets. They are typically low-maintenance and easy to train, and they love to mimic and sing. Budgies can live up to fifteen years.

**African gray parrots** are lauded for their ability to learn how to talk. Because of their intellect, they need people to interact with them regularly and puzzles and toys to play with, or else they start to develop behavioral problems. African grays can live up to forty years.

**Doves** are gentle and make calm companions. They require less attention than many other pet birds, making them ideal for owners with a busy schedule. They should be given time to fly around and so need a large cage or time to frolic in the home. Doves can live up to fifteen years.

**Conures** are mischievous clowns. They like to play around, perform tricks, and interact with their owners. These birds are quieter than other parrots and won't be able to mimic or learn speech, but their friendliness makes up for it. Conures can live up to thirty years.

**Lovebirds** are the smallest pet bird in the parrot family. They form loving bonds with their human owner and their mate. However, lovebirds will often try to assert dominance through aggression, making them less gentle than the others on this list. If properly cared for, they will live up to thirty years.

**Canaries** have been companions to humans for centuries (see page 77). They are shyer than other popular pet bird species and don't like to be handled, so it may be harder to establish a strong bond with them. However, male canaries are songsters and can brighten your home with their warbling. They can live up to ten years.

**Finches** are relatively quiet, independent pets. They aren't really fans of being handled, but they have a lot of energy. They do best when kept in pairs or small groups and can live up to ten years.

# Birds with Jobs

Birds have many talents. They can sing, navigate, and detect sounds and smells that we cannot, and they are deft hunters. Over the years, humans have harnessed these talents, employing birds to do various jobs that are otherwise difficult for people to perform.

## COAL MINE WARNING

"A canary in the coal mine" is a well-known saying meaning an early warning sign of a bigger problem. But the phrase is not just a metaphor. Canaries, yellow songbirds native to islands off the western coast of Africa—and popular modern-day pets—were used in the United Kingdom, Canada, and the United States beginning in the late 1800s to warn miners of the presence of poisonous gas.

The idea to employ canaries came from Scottish physician John Scott Haldane. In 1896, he was called in to investigate an explosion in a Welsh coal mine that led to the deaths of fifty-seven men. He determined the source of the incident was a buildup of carbon monoxide and suggested that animals be used to help detect levels of the gas, since they are more sensitive to it than humans.

The canary was singled out. They are small and

portable and, like all birds, have extremely sensitive lungs. Bird lungs are specially adapted with air sacs so that they can draw more oxygen from the air. Toxic gas, therefore, affects canaries long before humans.

For years, miners would carry canaries in special cages—designed with compartments that could revive the birds after gas poisoning—into their job sites. Miners often cared deeply about their canaries, whistling to them and treating them as companions. Eventually, the birds were phased out, replaced by electric sensors that can detect toxic underground fumes—although in some territories the birds are still kept as backup in case of electronic failure. It's believed that coal mine canaries have saved more than a million lives.

## PIGEON POST

Because of their navigation skills, ability to return to their roosts with perfect recall, and flight speed, pigeons have long been used to send messages. Homing pigeons can reach speeds greater than ninety miles per hour and can undertake journeys as long as six hundred miles.

Millennia ago, pigeon mail services were used in

Egypt and the Middle East, as well as in Greece, where the birds were used to communicate the winners of the ancient Olympics. Genghis Khan used pigeons to carry information on his military campaigns. By the 1800s, the practice became more widespread in the Western world, facilitating information exchange after the Industrial Revolution. In 1897, New Zealand established the Great Barrier Pigeongram, using the birds to send postage between Auckland and the Great Barrier Island. In Halifax, Nova Scotia, journalists used pigeons to send news to New York City from incoming European ships. During World War I and World War II, pigeons were also important messengers. Some even won awards for their service and were considered war heroes, including the following.

**Cher Ami:** This pigeon was one of the six hundred US Army Signal Corps pigeons sent to France to aid in World War I. The bird saved the Seventy-Seventh Division's "Lost Battalion" when they were trapped behind German lines, delivering a key message to American commanders alerting them to the location of the imperiled soldiers. He was awarded the prestigious Croix de Guerre medal for his service.

**Paddy:** Irish pigeon Paddy was the fastest pigeon to arrive back in the UK with the news of the successful D-Day invasion. The bird flew 230 miles in four hours and fifty minutes. He was awarded the Dickin Medal, a prize that was also awarded to thirty-one other pigeons, including Royal Blue, a male bird that was owned by King George VI and served with the Royal Air Force's National Pigeon Service.

**G. I. Joe:** The first American pigeon to receive the Dickin Medal, G. I. Joe helped save the residents of Calvi Vecchia in Italy during World War II. The town was supposed to be the target of an American air raid, but the British had won back the village from German forces ahead of schedule. This pigeon was able to get word to the US Air Force—journeying twenty miles in less than twenty minutes—to call off the attack.

Pigeon messengers are few and far between today. The last messaging system that used these birds was in India, where police departments in remote areas employed pigeons to send information during natural disasters. This last pigeon post service shuttered its doors in 2008.

Carrier pigeon G. I. Joe was awarded the Dickin Medal at the Tower of London in 1946.

## HONEY LOCATORS

In eastern Africa, humans long ago formed an unlikely partnership with the greater honeyguide, an unassuming brown bird with a pink bill. The collaboration has continued for millennia and benefits both species. Honeyguides know the location of bee colonies, but lack the skills to get to the beeswax they want to eat. Humans aren't as good at locating beehives, but are able to calm bees and break open hives, collecting the honey for themselves and their communities and leaving the wax behind for the birds.

The knowledge of honeyguides and how to work with them has been passed down for generations in this area of Africa. Each group has specific ways to communicate with the birds. When preparing for a honey hunt, the Yao people in Mozambique will give a loud trill followed by a grunt, while the Hadza group in Tanzania will emit a melodic whistle. Honeyguides will recognize this call, find the person giving the call, and lead them to their prize—a wonderful example of mutually beneficial human-bird collaboration.

## CORMORANT FISHING

Cormorants, which are long-necked fish-eating divers, have long been trained to catch fish for people. This practice has been best documented in China and Japan, but it has also been practiced in Peru, Greece, Macedonia, and even briefly in England and France. For thousands of years, fishermen have leashed cormorants, bringing them aboard boats. They tie a loose snare around the bird's neck, which prevents them from swallowing large fish (the cormorants can still eat small fish). They release the cormorants into the water. When a cormorant snags a large catch, the fisherman brings the bird back in, forcing it to regurgitate the fish.

Today, cormorant fishing has mostly been replaced by more modern and efficient methods. However, it is still practiced in Japan and China as a tourist attraction.

## FALCONRY

Although the exact origin of falconry is unknown, early records show that Central Asia and the Iranian plateau were hot spots for this practice. It began as a way for people to hunt by proxy: Raptors would catch small mammals or game birds and bring them back to their keepers. Over time, falconry became a sport and a cultural touchstone.

Falconry varies widely among locales and cultures, where the sport is adapted to different traditions and to the environment. For instance, in Kazakhstan, Kyrgyzstan, and Mongolia, some falconers train golden eagles to hunt large animals like foxes and wolves. Those on the Arabian Peninsula use the saker falcon, an important symbol in Arab culture. In Europe, falconers typically use kestrels or hawks.

Today, falconry is still an art form with an active community, carried on as a way to preserve cultural heritage and to advocate for the conservation of raptors.

## Invasive Birds

Like birds, humans are migratory and have traveled all around the globe. Often, the birds that have relationships with humans will follow them (or will be deliberately brought along or released) and learn to survive in new environments. This makes for all kinds of interesting stories, ranging from conflict with native fauna to peaceful coexistence.

On the conflict end of the spectrum, birds can be invasive species. Animals that are introduced to new places usually lack competition and natural predators, meaning that their populations will boom. This disrupts the delicate balance of ecosystems, causing a cascade of environmental issues.

For example, European starlings were introduced to North America in the late 1800s. Although the true origin of their established presence in the New World is still debated, the widely told story points back to a man named Eugene Schieffelin. He wanted to introduce all the birds mentioned in William Shakespeare's plays to New York's Central Park and released several starlings. He had to do this multiple times, after his early attempts failed.

Today, European starlings in North America form large flocks like they do in Europe. The most pressing concern is that they consume corn in livestock feed, damaging dairy farms. They also compete with native birds, taking over cavity nest sites and gobbling up food. In fact, their presence is so strong that they'll often displace native species like bluebirds. House sparrows, another introduced species from Europe that have become common in urban areas, will also aggressively push out other songbirds from feeding and nesting sites. This has earned both European starlings and house sparrows the label of invasive species.

But not all introduced birds threaten the balance of ecosystems. Pet parrots will often escape, establishing colonies far outside of their normal range. In the 1960s, a flock of monk parakeets, shipped up from the tropics and destined for pet stores, escaped from New York's John F. Kennedy Airport. This flock is thought to have settled in Brooklyn and has now been here for multiple generations, thriving despite the colder climate.

Similar stories have played out in places such as San Francisco, where a group of cherry-headed conures have made their home in Telegraph Hill to the delight of locals. Because of their limited damage to other species and the overall ecosystem, these parrots are considered *naturalized species*, a label that is used for non-native species that are self-sustaining but not destructive. Naturalized species also include other common organisms found in North America that were long ago introduced from Europe, such as earthworms and dandelions.

# Bird Lore: Avian Myths, Folklore, and Legends

It's no wonder that humans have long thought that birds are mysterious and magical. They fly. They sing. They sport beautiful colors. As a result, birds are prominent characters in many myths, legends, and superstitions around the world. Here are just a few.

## CLEVER RAVENS

In the United Kingdom, ravens are associated with the Tower of London. Legend has it that in the seventeenth century King Charles II, annoyed by the presence of the birds, ordered the removal of ravens from the premises. A series of misfortunes followed, leading the king to believe that it was because of his mistreatment of the ravens. He restored the birds' presence to the tower, where they still reside today. It's still believed that if these birds ever leave the Tower of London, it would be an omen that the safety of the kingdom is threatened. Today, the tower ravens are under the care of the Ravenmaster, who lets the ravens out during the day, cleans their cages, replenishes their water, and feeds them raw meat.

In Norse mythology, a pair of ravens called Huginn and Muninn are companions to the god Odin. They are thought to represent reflection, thought, and memory, and they whisper in Odin's ear. This has made him the wisest of the gods. Norse sailors also regarded ravens as sources of wisdom, using them as navigators while exploring northern seas.

In Native American myths, especially of the tribes on the Pacific Northwest coast, the raven is a trickster, able to shapeshift and manipulate to get what he needs. The raven is also a key figure in creation stories, although its exact role varies among Native American cultures.

## THIEVING MAGPIES

With their black heads, white bellies, and long, iridescent tail feathers, magpies are famous for being thieves of shiny objects. In folklore, their role is quite diverse around the world.

In China, the magpie is considered to be a symbol of good luck and happiness. Its name (xǐ què) literally translates to "happy bird." Similarly, Koreans believe that magpies deliver good news or indicate that kind visitors will be arriving soon.

In contrast, the magpie is often associated with bad luck in Europe. The presence of one magpie is a cause for sorrow in Britain, whereas a flock spells disaster. In Germany, the magpie is considered a bird of the underworld. In Scandinavia, it's thought that witches ride upon or turn into magpies.

Some Indigenous groups in North America consider magpies as loyal friends of humans, messengers that will warn them of danger. In particular, the magpie is a sacred messenger from the Creator for the Cheyenne and a guardian for Pueblo people. However, some legends from other Indigenous groups cast the bird more as a gossip or annoyance.

## WISE OWLS

Able to hunt at night, turn their heads in almost a full circle, and fly in silence, owls are widespread symbols in many cultures. They're often associated with death: The sight or sound of an owl in ancient Egypt is a signal that someone has died or will die. Owls were also said to foretell the deaths of several Caesars in ancient Rome.

In ancient Greece, the owl was a symbol of Athena, the goddess of wisdom, craft, and military strategy. In more recent times, owls are often wise characters in fiction. They are also associated with magic, as companions of witches and wizards in Arthurian legends and Harry Potter.

Owls are sometimes thought to bring good fortune. In Japan, images of owls are believed to ward off famine and epidemics. Owl feathers are worn by some Native Americans as a symbol of bravery and good luck.

## NOBLE EAGLES

Majestic, fearsome predators that soar high in the sky, eagles have inspired many myths around the world. In Arabic poetry, eagles are a symbol of power. In Celtic mythology, the eagle is old and wise. In Native American stories, the eagle is a medicine bird and plays a role in spiritual ceremonies.

Eagle feathers are highly prized in various cultures. Highland chiefs in Scotland wear three eagle feathers to signify their rank. They are also used in headdresses in ceremonies by various Native Americans on the Great Plains, such as the Lakota and Cheyenne, and are awarded for acts of bravery.

## LUCKY ALBATROSS

Albatross are large-winged seabirds that spend most of their lives wandering the oceans. They are good navigators, and sailors will often readjust their course to follow the birds. As a result, albatross are key characters in the myths of seagoing crews. The sight of an albatross is good luck. If no albatross is seen or, worse, a dead albatross is discovered, that is a sign that the journey is doomed.

## BLESSED BIRD POOP

Perhaps the most famous bird-related superstition is that a bird pooping on you is a sign of good luck. The belief is thought to have originated in Russia. Statistically speaking, the odds of a bird pooping on you are relatively low. You need to be in the right place at the right time, so luck is definitely needed. Although it's hard to tell if the saying is earnest or just a way to make you feel better about being soiled by bird droppings.

## SUPERSTITIONS AT A GLANCE

- In British folklore, a blackbird making a nest at your house is a sign of fortune.
- Tipping your hat at a magpie, according to British folklore, can bring you luck.
- Also according to British folklore, seeing five crows means that sickness is on its way.

- In some Native American folklore, a kingfisher is a lucky bird.
- Sparrows carry the souls of the dead. This folklore stems from many cultures, including ancient Egypt.
- According to medieval European folklore, wrens can prevent drowning.
- A bird that flies into your house is an important messenger in Celtic folklore. If it dies, or is white, it means that it is foretelling death.

## BIRD IDIOMS

There are a lot of sayings associated with birds. Some make intuitive sense or are derived from history. Others just demonstrate how silly language can be.

**To have an albatross around one's neck:** Referring to a burden or a cursed fate. Based on Samuel Taylor Coleridge's 1798 poem "The Rime of the Ancient Mariner," in which a sailor dooms his crew by killing an albatross and is forced to face his mistake by wearing the bird around his neck.

**Dead as a dodo:** Used to emphasize that something or someone is very dead. This saying derives from the fact that the dodo was once a plentiful and popular game bird on the island nation of Mauritius. However, due to overhunting by passing sailors and the introduction of invasive species, the dodo quickly became extinct in the late seventeenth century.

**As the crow flies:** The shortest straight-line distance between one location and another. It was once believed that crows fly in a direct line, based on observations of crows traveling alone and with purpose across the open countryside. But in reality, crows do like to take detours and will circle above their nests and roosts.

**Crazy as a loon:** The word *loon* is used to describe someone who is considered crazy or foolish. Surprisingly, it's derived neither from the word *lunatic* nor from the bird's haunting yodel—which people often describe as sounding like the laugh of a crazy person. Instead, it has an unrelated origin in old Scottish and British English.

**Talk turkey:** To talk about business or a serious matter. According to one theory, this idiom arose in colonial America, where pilgrims would often discuss turkeys with Native Americans as a part of trade agreements.

**Happy as a lark:** When someone is cheerful or content. This saying is likely is connected with the lark's song, which is melodic and joyous. It's a song that's often referred to in historical records, as well as in the plays of William Shakespeare.

**A cuckoo in the nest:** When there is an unwelcome intruder. Cuckoos are brood parasites (see page 45) and will lay their eggs in nests of other species.

**Goosebumps:** Bumps on your skin that appear when you're cold, which look like the skin of a goose when it is plucked. Also referred to as *goose pimples*, depending on where you are.

**Hoodwinked:** When someone has been scammed or tricked. This word comes from a practice in falconry in which falconers put hoods on the heads of falcons to cover their eyes, which keeps the birds calm.

## AUGURY

In ancient Rome, birds were believed to be important omens. The religious practice of reading these omens was called *augury*. An official known as an augur was trained to note bird movements and read their behavior to predict the future. These observations were called *auspices*. Often, augurs were consulted before important government decisions were made. If the decision misinterpreted or ignored the auspice, then the anger of the gods would be invoked, a consequence that many hoped to avoid.

# BIRD-
## WATCHING
## AND BEYOND

# How to Bird-Watch (and Why)

For a beginner, getting into bird-watching can be daunting. Field guides are full of birds you don't know and terminology that you're unfamiliar with. A lot of birding walks, too, can feel intimidating. It seems that everyone else has seen that bird before or knows what's going on—except for you.

But birding doesn't have to be overwhelming. If you've ever seen a bird and wondered what it was, or even just enjoyed the peaceful chatter of the birds through your kitchen window, that's bird-watching. It doesn't have to be about identifying as many rare species as possible or knowing all the birdsongs—although it can be, if that's your thing!

So instead of telling you how to bird-watch in one specific way—because bird-watching is as unique as the individual doing it—I have a couple of general tips that I wish someone told me when I started. Maybe they'll be helpful in some way to you too.

## BE OBSERVANT

Because birding is so accessible, the first step is to get outside—or even just look out the window—and take in everything around you. It doesn't matter if you're in the middle of the wilderness or on a bench in a city park; wherever you may be, birds are there too. Look for birds, but also listen for their songs and watch their interactions. Note if they're sleeping or preening or bathing or looking for food.

Over time, you'll start to see patterns. You'll notice that Canada geese are not usually alone and get aggressively territorial when other groups approach. If you've set up a bird feeder, you might notice that blue jays tend to dominate, pushing all other birds away with their presence. You may notice that black-capped chickadees are especially curious. All of these observations and quirks can also help you remember and learn species, in addition to learning and looking for their markings. So just get out there and look at some birds! If you approach with curiosity, it's impossible not to learn something.

## CHOOSE YOUR FIELD GUIDE WISELY

Field guides are the surefire way for you to learn your bird species, but it's important to choose one that makes the most sense for you. If you're mostly looking at birds in your backyard, then a backyard-bird-specific guide may be a good starting point. Similarly, regional bird guides can help you narrow down species you may be seeing when you're first starting out, pointing you to the most common birds in your area. That being said, national or continental field guides (the standard range for them) are helpful to have, especially once you've learned to recognize the common culprits in your area and you start traveling to new locales with unfamiliar faces.

Digital field guides are also a great, convenient resource, as they are usually already sorted by geographic location. The Merlin app by the Cornell Lab of Ornithology is a great option. Just make sure your location is turned on, otherwise you'll get suggestions of birds from the other side of the world.

## FIND YOUR GROUP

One of the quickest ways to learn your birds is to lean on the expertise of other birders. Everyone's accumulated their own identification tricks throughout the years, and some might stick in your brain better than others.

However, not all birding groups are created equal. As with field guides, there are choices you can make here. Some groups or birding walks are specifically designed for beginners, and they teach the ropes of identification. If your goal is just vibes—learning about birds through osmosis—or if you're not really a person who wants to hike for hours, there are groups designed for that too! (See "Further Resources" on page 141.)

And finally, if you have enough bird-interested friends around you to do so, you can form your own informal birding group.

But if you prefer to bird alone, that's fine, too—one of the best parts about birding can be getting a break from other humans!

## TAKE YOUR TIME

There are a lot of birds. Many of them look the same and sound the same, so it's important to take your time. In your first year, focus on observing the birds in your neighborhood. By the second year, if you feel ready, you can broaden your horizons and start to learn how bird species can vary throughout the seasons.

Taking your time can allow you to learn more, not just about birds and their yearly and seasonal cycles, but also the ecosystems that we share with them, as well as our own place within them. There's no shortcut to becoming an expert at these things, other than continually noticing birds—even if that's just on your walk to the grocery store. And once you make a habit of observing the world around you, who knows what else you might notice?

## BIRDING BENEFITS

Birding became a popular activity for good reason. Studies have shown that watching birds, hearing their songs, and experiencing the diversity of birdlife can increase happiness, help people recover from stress, and even rewire your brain. Birding has even been suggested by therapists as an alternative to meditation, since it requires you to sit still and observe the world around you. In recent years, slow birding—the practice of staying in one spot to watch birds—has become quite popular.

If you've begun birding, you may have already noticed these brain benefits. Maybe you've become more mindful and learned to slow down or simply found joy in watching a mockingbird hop among the trees. In short, there's not really a downside to bird-watching, no matter how slow, or how fast, you take it.

## Birder Lingo to Know

Birders have a lot of weird terms for things. You might encounter some of these terms throughout your bird-watching journey, or maybe completely different ones! Birder slang is constantly changing, and some terms may be specific to individual birding communities.

Here's a not-so-comprehensive list of birding terminology to know. I also highly encourage you to create your own slang—things are just more fun that way!

**Big day:** A birding event in which birders try to spot as many species as they can in a single day.

**Big year:** Similar to a big day, a person may declare a big year if they're trying to see as many species as possible in a year. It's also the title of a famous birding movie.

**Bins:** The shortened version of binoculars. Best used like so: *Hey, have you seen my bins?*

**Birder:** A bird-watcher: a person who observes or identifies birds.

**CBC:** The Christmas Bird Count, an annual volunteer bird census conducted by the National Audubon Society that has been ongoing since 1900.

**Chase:** To pursue a rare bird.

**Dip:** When you missed out on seeing a bird that you really wanted to see. Best used in a sentence like: *Aw, man, I dipped on that great gray owl.*

**Fallout:** When a hoard of migratory birds are forced down to the ground due to inclement weather. Usually occurs in the spring, sometimes in the fall.

**FOY:** First of year. In other words, the first time you've seen a particular bird species in a new year.

**LBJ:** Little brown job. Refers to any bird that is small and brown. There are a lot of them!

**Lifer:** A bird you haven't seen before—a new one for your life list.

**Lister:** A hardcore version of a birder: someone who chases rare birds and has a singular goal of expanding their list. In the UK, this is referred to as a *twitcher*.

**Jizz (or giss):** The general vibes of a bird. In a sentence: *Based on the jizz, I think that bird was a red-tailed hawk.*

**Megararity:** A bird that got really, really lost and ended up in some place where they aren't supposed to be. It might be the only time this species has ever been seen in a particular place.

**Nemesis bird:** A bird that you have dipped on over and over again. It feels like everyone else has seen it except for you at this point.

**Patch:** The local area that you most often bird-watch in.

**Peeps:** Small sandpipers that all basically look the same.

**Pelagic:** A marathon boat trip that birders take to see seabirds that are rarely found near shore. Also describes birds that spend a lot of time on the ocean.

**Pish:** A *psh-psh-psh* sound that birders make to catch the attention of small birds. It sounds like an alarm call of many species, so it gets birds out in the open because they want to see what all the hubbub is about.

**Scope:** A spotting scope, which is a small telescope you can carry around to look at faraway birds. Also can be used as a verb, like so: *I'm gonna scope this area for rare gulls.*

**SOB (spouse of birder):** The person who unfortunately (or fortunately?) has to deal with their partner's birding obsession.

**Spark bird:** The bird that started your birding obsession.

**Spuh:** Refers to *sp.*, as in the notation for an unknown species. In a sentence: *Oh, that's a gull spuh. I don't know which species.*

**Usual suspects:** The usual birds you see, nothing too exciting. Something you can answer when someone asks what you saw: *Any good birds today? Just the usual suspects.*

**Vagrant:** A bird that has, again, gotten very, very lost. Rare, but not as rare as a megararity.

**Warbler neck:** The pain you feel in your neck after spending too much time looking at the treetops for warblers.

**Yard list:** The list of birds you've seen in your backyard.

# Identifying Birds

When you first see a bird, begin your identification by observing its size, shape, and habitat. If you're still unsure, try some more advanced tactics, such as the ones described below.

## SIZE AND SHAPE

When first approaching an unknown bird, note its size and general shape. Is it larger than a crow? Is it shaped more like a duck, or a small songbird? Doing so can narrow down your options considerably, since size and shape can help you zero in on the appropriate bird group to look at (see "Bird Families" on page 14).

Details of a bird's shape can also tell you more about what it is. Does it have a crest? Is the bill short and stout, or long and thin? Looking at the details can help you narrow things down to species level.

## HABITAT

Pay attention to *where* you are seeing the bird. Is it high up in a tree? Foraging in the mud by the water? If it's the latter, you may have a shorebird in your sights. Some birds are also habitat specialists. For example, eastern bluebirds tend to be on the edges of open habitats like fields and meadows.

## BEHAVIOR

Take some time to note what the bird is doing. Is it creeping along the tree bark? Then it may be a brown creeper. Is it perched on a bare branch and hunting insects? Then it may be a type of flycatcher. (Reviewing "Foraging" on page 46 may help with this.) Noting if the bird is alone or in a flock can also help you identify it.

## TIME OF YEAR

As we noted with bird migration, bird movements and locales are often seasonal. Most field guides will show a range map for a bird and where they are found in each season. For example, dark-eyed juncos are a characteristic winter bird in most parts of North America, as that is when they leave their breeding grounds, usually at higher elevations.

## FIELD MARKS

Look in any field guide, and it will talk about field marks—distinctive colors, stripes, or patterns on a specific part of a bird. The jargon around these gets quite technical, but such marks can be helpful when you're looking at very similar birds (like when you really can't figure out an identification). For example, chipping sparrows have an orangey crown and paler face that distinguishes them from other sparrows. Sparrows are hard to differentiate, so be patient when identifying them. Bay-breasted warblers have very bright white wing bars (fall warblers are also an identification challenge!) as do northern mockingbirds.

To get you started on understanding field marks, learn some bird anatomy terms so that you can get more precise when describing a bird's appearance.

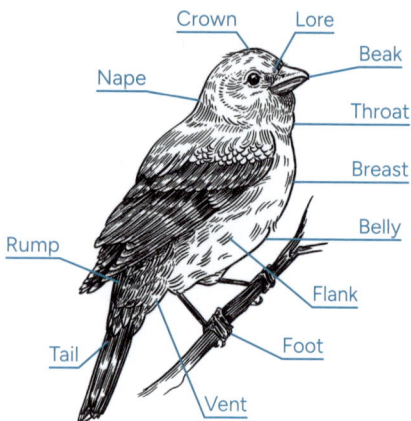

Crown · Lore · Beak · Nape · Throat · Breast · Belly · Rump · Flank · Tail · Foot · Vent

## SOUND

A bird's song or call can also give away its identity. A general impression of a bird's call can help with initial narrowing of identification choices. For example: Is it a quacking duck, or a shrieking raptor, or a musical songbird? More subtle differences in songs and calls are especially helpful with songbirds, since this group has such diverse sounds.

If you're really dedicated, you can memorize bird-songs and learn to recognize them in the field. Birders listen to a lot of songs over and over again to learn this skill and come up with clever mnemonics to remember specific songs. Some birds will also conveniently appear to say their names while singing (such as peewees, chickadees, and killdeer). This is called *onomatopoeia*.

But nowadays, technology makes it relatively easy to identify bird songs. The app Merlin is a birdcall identification app that can translate the songs it hears into possible bird IDs—although it's recommended to confirm your identification by observing the actual bird instead of relying on the app alone.

## IF YOU SPOT A RARE BIRD

If you're one of the lucky birders to spot a vagrant or a megararity, you can report your sighting to your local bird club or post it to the citizen science platform eBird. It helps to collect documentation, like photos or sound recordings, to make sure your identification is rock-solid.

Every rare bird report is carefully reviewed by a committee of expert birders. It's not uncommon to get rejected; these reports have a high bar! But if your sighting passes the threshold, it will be added to state or county bird records, where it may catch the excitement of the birding community, including the American Birding Association's Rare Bird Alert.

# Tools and Supplies

One of the best things about birding is that all you need to participate are your senses. But if you're looking to level up your practice, a few handy tools can help enhance your bird-watching experience.

## BINOCULARS

Binoculars, in my humble opinion, are optional in birding. But they do enhance the experience, so if you are deep enough into birding to want to invest in a pair, I would highly recommend it.

In general, you shouldn't have to shell out thousands of dollars for a good pair of binoculars (or should I say bins?). A decent pair usually costs around $200 to $300. It's worth going to a physical store and trying some out. See what feels good, or ask a friend if you can borrow their binoculars for a test drive.

Binoculars have numbers (for example, 8×32 or 10×40) that distinguish them. The first number is the magnification. The bigger the number, the greater the magnification. The second number is the size of the lens—the smaller the number, the narrower and darker the lens.

Although it may seem like you would want maximum magnification with the widest lens, those binoculars get very heavy very quickly. The most popular configurations are 10×42 and 8×42, which are popular for a good reason and make good starting points. Brands like Vortex, Nikon, Bushnell, and Celestron are popular beginner options.

## SCOPES

A spotting scope is like a small telescope: something you can put on a tripod to look at stationary birds far out in the water or in a field, like ducks, gulls, or owls. Typically, more experienced birders will have a scope, which you might notice if you join a birding walk. If you feel like your binoculars keep coming up short or that you would benefit from seeing greater detail, consider investing in a scope.

## CAMERAS

A camera can be a great companion to bird-watching. Some birders carry only cameras rather than binoculars in order to document what they see. This is especially helpful for building your list out on eBird. Digital point-and-shoot cameras have great zoom capabilities nowadays. Or if you're feeling more serious, you could invest in a DSLR with a large telephoto lens.

## FIELD GUIDES AND NOTEBOOKS

A pocket-sized field guide (or a digital one on your phone) is a great tool to have in the field (see "How to Bird-Watch" on page 98). You could also keep a larger copy in your car or at home for reference.

In addition to a field guide, you might find it useful to carry a notebook to take notes while you're birding, especially if you're on a solo observation session. (Rite in the Rain makes good waterproof field notebooks.)

## SUPPLIES CHECKLIST

Here's a handy-dandy checklist, useful for any outdoor excursion:

- Binoculars
- Snacks
- Water (and/or other beverages)
- Hat (in the summer: brimmed; in the winter: warm)
- Weather-appropriate gear (for example, windbreaker, sunscreen, gloves, extra layers, etc.)
- Fully charged phone
- Field guide

# Common Backyard Birds

Throughout North America, you'll likely see some recurring familiar faces in your backyard. These species are great places to start when you're building your bird identification skills.

## AMERICAN ROBIN

The esteemed songster of the backyard, American robins are usually the first ones belting their songs in the morning and the last ones singing at night. They can be identified by their characteristic red breast (darker in males, lighter in females). When not singing, the American robin can be found foraging on grassy lawns during the breeding season, where they run, pause to look for worms, and pounce when their prey is in sight. In the colder months, robins gather in large flocks, flying from one tasty berry bush to the next.

## MOURNING DOVE

The sad, owllike *cooo-OOOO-ooo-ooo-ooo* of the mourning dove is a song many are familiar with. These small doves are common backyard residents for most of eastern North America, where they perch on branches, power lines, and fences. Their plumage is a soft chestnut, and they'll often come down to the ground to forage for seeds. In fact, mourning doves are seed specialists (granivores)—grains make up 99 percent of their diet. When frightened, these plucky birds will take off in a frenzy, their wings whistling with every beat.

## NORTHERN MOCKINGBIRD

Although it may sound like you're hearing a bird, car alarm, and creaky gate in quick succession, all of those noises may be made by the northern mockingbird. This gray bird is an expert mimic, a skill shared by many in the Mimidae family. In fact, they can often fool birdsong ID apps like Merlin, so make sure to listen closely: Mockingbirds often repeat their songs at least three times, so they will reveal their identity as their serenade continues. You may also find these birds chasing others, as they are quite territorial. In doing so, they will soar, flashing their white wing patches while in flight.

## WHITE-BREASTED NUTHATCH

If you see a tiny bird acrobatically creeping down a tree, it may be a white-breasted nuthatch. These plucky birds are tree specialists. They'll snag invertebrates out of the tree bark and cache large seeds in the crevices. If

Black-capped chickadee

American robin

Dark-eyed junco

Northern mockingbird

American goldfinch

Mourning dove

White-breasted nuthatch

Song sparrow

a nuthatch is particularly chatty, it will quite literally be yammering away. Listen for this *yank-yank* call so that you can sneak a peek at their slate-blue backs, black caps, and white bellies.

## AMERICAN GOLDFINCH

Seeing an American goldfinch is always a joy. These birds are bright yellow in the spring and summer, and males have a stark black crown. Their voices are cheery, letting out a bouncy *po-ta-to-chiiip* when in flight. Goldfinches are also seed specialists. In the autumn and winter—when they've molted into their more muted winter plumages—goldfinches can be found flocking on the dried seed heads of various plants and flowers.

## DOWNY WOODPECKER

The smallest woodpecker in North America, the downy woodpecker is also the most common woodpecker seen in backyards. They typically hang out in forested areas, drilling into stands of dead wood for tasty invertebrates and sounding off a bright *pik* or whinny. These little birds can be identified by their striped face, black speckled back, white belly, and characteristic upright pose. Males will also have a red spot on the back of their heads (their nape). They can be confused with their larger and similar-looking relative, the hairy woodpecker, which is less common but not impossible to find.

## DARK-EYED JUNCO

These little sparrows typically forage on the ground for seeds. They can be identified by their dark gray head, soft pink bill, and bright white tail feathers, which they'll flash when in flight. The colors of these birds can vary depending on where you are. There are a total of fifteen subspecies of juncos, which are generally lumped into six groups. The most common is the slate-colored, the subspecies found in much of eastern North America, which has a gray back and white belly. But many dark-eyed juncos in the Rocky Mountains and on the West Coast have various patterns of brown, white, and gray.

## HOUSE FINCH

Male house finches look as if their head and chest were dipped in raspberry jam. Their brown streaky bodies stand in direct contrast with the bright reds in the rest of their plumage. Females do not have as much color, but still look elegant with their deep brown plumage.

They'll frequent feeders in small flocks, using their thick, conical bills to crack open seeds. In spring, you may hear their long, twittering, cheery song.

## SONG SPARROW

This is one of the most common brown streaky sparrows in North America, and likely the first LBJ (a.k.a. little brown job; see "Birder Lingo to Know," page 103) you'll see in a shrubby or marshy area. In the breeding season, the song sparrow will often perch out in the open, singing two to three spaced-out notes followed by a bubbly song and ending with a buzzy trill. This is another sparrow with substantial regional variations in color. Song sparrows in Alaska are noticeably darker and larger than ones further south, while ones in the Southwest are relatively pale.

## BLACK-CAPPED CHICKADEE

Perhaps the most friendly and curious of all backyard birds, the black-capped chickadee is a familiar face. With their namesake black cap, these birds look adorable because of their disproportionately large heads. They're acrobatic, sometimes hanging upside down while flitting from branch to branch. They're usually the first to locate a new bird feeder.

BRINGING

BIRDS TO YOU

# Making Bird-Friendly Habitats

Whether you have a backyard or balcony, there are ways to make your space into a flourishing habitat for birds. Providing this habitat can not only attract local residents, but can also be a critical source of food and water for migrants to stop at and refuel.

The basic idea of a bird-friendly habitat is to create a place where a variety of birds can find food, water, and shelter. There are a few ways to do this.

## PLANT NATIVE PLANTS

The best way to provide your backyard birds with the best food is to plant native plants. Try to choose a variety that will offer food sources year-round. Here are some food sources to consider:

**Insects:** Native trees like oaks and maples and plants like goldenrod and milkweed provide perfect homes for insect larvae in the summer, which can be a bonanza for birds in warmer months.

**Seeds and nuts:** Seed-producing plants like cone-flowers and sunflowers are a great source of food for seed-loving birds in the fall and winter. Trees like oaks and walnuts can also be a source of fat- and protein-rich nuts, which birds can cache for the colder seasons.

**Fruit:** Try to look for plants that produce berries or other fruits, like plums, cherries, and more, which can service birds throughout the year.

**Nectar:** Hummingbirds drink nectar, so it's a good idea to plant tubular red or pink flowers like currants and columbine to attract them. Aster flowers are also great for various insect pollinators, while providing seeds for birds in the fall.

When choosing native plants for your habitat, it's helpful to select a variety of different heights. This will create what are called *habitat layers* in your backyard, rather than a uniform lawn, which can also help attract different birds. For instance, warblers that tend to forage high up will gravitate toward trees, whereas lower-lying shrubs can be good hiding and foraging spots for ground-dwelling species like sparrows.

For balcony owners or those who don't have a lot outdoor space, look for compact plants that thrive in a variety of conditions, like goldenrod, milkweed, and black-eyed Susans.

## BE A GOOD STEWARD

For your backyard to be bird-friendly, it's important to take care of the habitat. This means you should:

- Remove invasive plants, which can crowd out the native plants that birds prefer.
- Refrain from using insecticides, since insects are the primary food source for many birds.
- Keep raking to a minimum. Leaving leaves behind can provide habitat for invertebrates, which are both pollinators and a key source of nutrients for many birds. Leaf cover also provides a natural mulch for plants, and it can reduce weeds!
- Keep dead trees standing (if you can do so safely). They could be a future home for woodpeckers or other cavity-nesting birds. Keeping other dead vegetation around, such as seed heads and stumps, can also provide an additional food source for birds—as well as natural mulch when they eventually rot away.

## INTRODUCE OTHER FEATURES

To take your backyard to the next level, you can also take some time to build or install extra features. This will further support birds in all parts of their life and seasonal cycles.

**Make a brush pile:** A brush pile is a pile of stacked logs and branches. Some birds will forage and even nest in these structures. Brush piles also serve as important habitats for small mammals, amphibians, insects, and reptiles.

**Place nest boxes:** Nest boxes, once installed, can be a great place for cavity nesters like bluebirds, chickadees, swallows, and more to raise the next generation. You can opt to build your own nest boxes (there are schematics online) or purchase them from a local hardware store.

**Put up a bird bath:** Providing a water source for birds can be especially helpful during hot days. You can also add a fountain or bubbler: Birds are attracted to the sound of moving water, so adding this feature can help birds locate the bath. Most birds prefer shallow water; one to two inches deep is ideal.

# Bird Feeding 101

Before we break down the different food types that are involved with bird feeding, it's important to set some ground rules.

Bird feeding is an ethical dilemma, since you're introducing an external source of food that may have unintended consequences. Bringing birds together at a feeder leaves them vulnerable to disease and predators. It can also shift bird behavior once they learn that feeders are a reliable source of nourishment. Studies have shown that birds such as Carolina wrens and Anna's hummingbirds have shifted their ranges northward due to the presence of feeders, since these human inputs provide food in the otherwise barren landscapes of winter. On the other hand, having food available year-round means that birds are able to stick around in the cold and establish breeding territories earlier in the spring. Some researchers posit that bird feeding helps birds survive in the face of habitat loss, climate change, and other human-driven challenges.

All that is to say, if you do choose to put out bird feeders, it is a responsibility. Make sure to:

• Keep feeders clean! Dirty feeders can transmit disease.

- Look out for predators. If cats, bears, or other large animals frequent your feeders, it might be best to take them down.
- Reduce window collisions by placing feeders within three feet of windows. At this distance, birds won't be able to gain enough momentum to injure themselves if they fly into a window. You can also put decals on your windows to break up reflections.
- And remember, native plants are also a great source of food for birds.

Of course, bird feeding isn't just about giving them food. It's about becoming more familiar with the residents and visitors of our backyards. In a sense, we need bird feeders more than birds do. It's a source of joy. So it's important we don't harm birds in the process.

## TYPES OF BIRD FEEDERS

There are many types of bird feeders. Selecting the right one depends on which species you're hoping to attract (or avoid) and which feeder style is the best fit for your outdoor space and lifestyle. Here are some of the most common types of feeders.

**Platform:** A flat platform. Platforms can attract a wide variety of birds, such as doves, grosbeaks, and quail, in addition to the usual suspects (see "Common Backyard Birds," page 116). They can get dirty quickly, are exposed to rain or snow, and are susceptible to squirrel raids.

**House:** A little hanging house that has a roof to keep seed dry and clean. However, seed can still get wet and is easily accessible by squirrels and other mammals.

**Tube:** A plastic tube with openings throughout. Because the seed is enclosed in the tube, the food is kept clean and dry. However, the smaller perches on this feeder make it best suited for small songbirds like finches. The small perches also do not deter squirrels, who may chew holes in the plastic.

**Window:** A feeder that you can suction cup onto your window, making for great viewing opportunities for you (or your indoor cat!). It typically is best for small birds like chickadees or titmice and is close enough to the window to deter collisions. Attaching this feeder, however, can be tricky.

**Nyjer:** A metal mesh tube with various perches and openings. This feeder is especially designed for nyjer seed, which is favored by finches, redpolls, and buntings. Squirrels aren't attracted to nyjer seed, so they will be less of a problem.

**Suet:** A rectangular wire cage that can hold a block of suet. (Alternately, you can simply smear the thick concoction onto a piece of wood.) Suet is high in fat and energy and may attract less common birds like woodpeckers, nuthatches, or even warblers. Because suet goes bad quickly, especially in hot weather, this type of feeder needs to be cleaned very regularly.

**Orange feeders:** A house feeder with hooks on which you can impale orange halves. These feeders are specifically designed for orioles and other fruit-loving birds.

**Hummingbird feeders:** A hanging feeder that is typically a glass bottle and often red, a color that attracts hummingbirds. Human-made "nectar" is put in these feeders, which is made from water and granulated sugar.

## HUMMINGBIRD NECTAR RECIPE

To make nectar, mix 4 parts water and 1 part sugar together. Stir to dissolve the sugar, then bring the mixture to a boil. Wait for it to cool completely before filling the feeder. The sugar water can spoil easily and needs to be regularly replaced. There's no need to add red food coloring or honey to the nectar, and these ingredients are harmful to the birds.

## TYPES OF BIRD FOOD

When purchasing bird food, you may become overwhelmed by all the options. Here are some of the most common bird food types.

**Mixed seed:** A safe bet—usually a mix of millet, sunflower, peanuts, corn and other seeds.

**Sunflower seeds:** A favorite of many birds, including chickadees and nuthatches. There are two types of sunflower seeds, black oil and striped. Black oil has a thinner shell and high fat content, and so is favored by many birds. Striped sunflower has a thicker shell, suited for birds with stronger seed-cracking abilities.

**Millet:** Not as broadly popular, but preferred by dark-eyed juncos and other sparrows.

**Peanuts:** Blue jays love these, as do white-breasted nuthatches.

**Nyjer seed:** A favorite of finches such as the American goldfinch, pine siskin, and redpoll.

**Suet:** An amalgamation of fat and seeds. Preferred by woodpeckers.

**Safflower seeds:** Thick-shelled seeds preferred by cardinals, grosbeaks, and chickadees.

**Mealworms:** For protein-seeking birds like eastern bluebirds. (Put these in glass, metal, or plastic feeders. Wooden feeders will get chewed through.)

**Fruit:** Oranges can be placed out for Baltimore orioles in the spring and summer.

See page 134 for a handy-dandy chart showing which foods are best for which birds.

| | MIXED SEED | BLACK SUNFLOWER SEED | MILLET | PEANUTS |
|---|---|---|---|---|
| **AMERICAN GOLDFINCH** | ● | ● | ○ | ○ |
| **BALTIMORE ORIOLE** | ○ | ○ | ○ | ○ |
| **BLACK-CAPPED CHICKADEE** | ● | ● | ○ | ○ |
| **BLUE JAY** | ● | ● | ○ | ● |
| **DARK-EYED JUNCO** | ● | ● | ○ | ● |
| **DOWNY WOODPECKER** | ● | ● | ○ | ● |
| **EASTERN BLUEBIRD** | ○ | ○ | ○ | ○ |
| **EVENING GROSBEAK** | ● | ○ | ○ | ○ |
| **GRAY CATBIRD** | ○ | ○ | ○ | ○ |
| **HOUSE FINCH** | ● | ● | ○ | ○ |
| **MOURNING DOVE** | ● | ● | ● | ○ |
| **NORTHERN CARDINAL** | ● | ● | ○ | ○ |
| **RED-BREASTED NUTHATCH** | ● | ● | ○ | ● |
| **REDPOLL** | ○ | ○ | ○ | ○ |
| **SONG SPARROW** | ● | ● | ● | ○ |
| **TUFTED TITMOUSE** | ● | ● | ○ | ● |
| **WHITE-BREASTED NUTHATCH** | ● | ● | ○ | ● |

| NYJER SEED | SUET | SAFFLOWER SEEDS | MEALWORMS | FRUIT |
|:---:|:---:|:---:|:---:|:---:|
| ● | ○ | ○ | ○ | ○ |
| ○ | ○ | ○ | ○ | ● |
| ○ | ● | ● | ● | ○ |
| ○ | ● | ○ | ○ | ○ |
| ● | ○ | ○ | ○ | ○ |
| ○ | ● | ○ | ○ | ○ |
| ○ | ○ | ○ | ● | ○ |
| ○ | ○ | ● | ○ | ○ |
| ○ | ○ | ○ | ● | ● |
| ● | ○ | ● | ○ | ○ |
| ● | ○ | ● | ○ | ○ |
| ○ | ○ | ● | ● | ○ |
| ○ | ● | ○ | ● | ○ |
| ● | ○ | ○ | ○ | ○ |
| ○ | ○ | ○ | ○ | ○ |
| ○ | ○ | ○ | ● | ○ |
| ○ | ● | ○ | ● | ○ |

# What to Do If You Find an Injured Bird

When you encounter an injured bird, it's natural to want to take the bird in and nurse it back to health. But there are many federal laws around handling wildlife, especially migratory birds or at-risk species, so approach the situation with care. Handle it like you would any unfolding emergency. The main goal is to make sure that the bird gets the best possible care so that it can continue its life in the wild.

## ASSESS THE SCENE

Look at the bird's surroundings. Is there anything that could have caused an injury? Is there a fallen nest? Is it near a window?

Then take a look at the bird itself. Does it have any visible injury, like a drooping wing or blood smear? Does it look alert or drowsy and unresponsive?

These are all details that you can use to determine what happened. Maybe the bird ran into the window and is suffering head trauma. Maybe it's a fledgling that just left the nest a little early.

In most cases, it's important to leave the bird alone and to relay information to a wildlife rehabilitation center if needed (they may also give you additional tips on what to do). If the bird isn't moving, or if it's at risk of being attacked by predators, hit by cars, or being trampled on, you can attempt to pick it up and place it in a cloth bag, box, or paper bag with air holes and lined with paper towels. This way it's protected until the wildlife rehabilitators arrive on the scene, or until it recovers on its own. Do not give the bird food or water—and be wary to keep yourself protected as well. If you take the risk of handling a bird, you may get bit or come into contact with avian flu.

If there doesn't appear to be a life-threatening injury, monitor the situation. If the bird continues to look sick or their health worsens after a few hours, then give a call to the professionals so that they can pick up the bird and treat it accordingly.

## WHO TO CALL

A quick web search of local licensed wildlife rehabilitation centers can be a good place to start. Most have phone numbers that you can call with an emergency, describe the situation, and arrange for pickup. In the United States, federal and state conservation agencies may provide a list of rehabs. Animal hospitals and vets may also be able to take wildlife patients, but call ahead to make sure.

## IF YOU FIND A BABY BIRD OUTSIDE OF ITS NEST

Baby birds often fall out of the nest. If possible, put the chick back into its nest. If you can't find the nest, then leave the bird alone or move it to a shaded area if needed. Again, monitor the situation. If the bird is exceedingly young and its parents haven't returned for a long time, give your local wildlife rehab a call.

As for bigger nestlings, who usually have more feathers and developed wings, don't worry about them if they look healthy otherwise. Fledglings will often leave the nest without well-developed flying abilities. They'll hang around the nest, and their parents will come back to feed them. Fledglings will eventually fly off on their own.

## Speaking Up for Birds

Although we've discussed a variety of actions that you can take to help birds, sometimes making bird-friendly habitats and caring for individual birds isn't quite enough. Sometimes we need to take a stand and speak up for birds, especially when policies and development in our cities, states, and countries threaten their future existence.

Diving into policy and law is daunting, especially because dynamics around conservation are often complex. There are many different voices and needs within our communities, so it's important to consider all of them. But as a bird person, you can lend your own viewpoints and values to these discussions.

Your voice can help sway a decision-maker. Make a call or write a letter to your representative. If you don't quite know where you start, your local conservation organizations may already have campaigns for a specific policy action or workshops on how to start lobbying and how to tell your story. You may even make fulfilling human connections with other bird lovers along the way.

If there's one thing to take away from this book, it's that that the fate and future of birds is ultimately linked with our stewardship of the environment, political actions, and education of ourselves and others. Inadvertently, our actions as a society affect birds and the places they live, just as birds affect our own lives. And sometimes, speaking up can have tangible impacts. Landmark laws for conservation, like the Migratory Bird Treaty Act, the Wild Bird Conservation Act, and the Bald and Golden Eagle Protection Act, have led to the recovery of many North American birds. This legislation—as well as potential future ones—needs continued support to make our world a better place for both birds and humans. We all play a part in this bigger system. And it's okay to start small—or, as Anne Lamott wrote, "bird by bird."

# Further Resources

## BIRDING GROUPS AND GENERAL RESOURCES

### Cornell Lab of Ornithology | *birds.cornell.edu*

One of the leading research institutions on ornithology in the United States. They also run eBird, All About Birds, and Birds of the World.

- ### eBird | *ebird.org*
  If you want to submit checklists for citizen science or just find out what people are seeing in your area (or someplace you're traveling to), eBird is a great place to start your search.
- ### All About Birds | *allaboutbirds.org*
  A comprehensive guide to birds in North America—including bird-watching resources.
- ### Birds of the World | *birdsoftheworld.org*
  A comprehensive guide to birds all over the world.

### National Audubon Society | *audubon.org*

A nonprofit for bird conservation. There are also many local and state Audubon chapters, some of which have switched out the Audubon name for Bird Alliance.

Find your nearest chapter at: www.audubon.org /about/chapters.

Audubon also has a native plants database, where you can search for native plants by zip code to find the best fit for your area: www.audubon.org/native-plants.

## American Birding Association (ABA) | *aba.org*

A good place to look for birding resources. This conservation nonprofit has a code of birding ethics, rare bird designations, a rare bird alert, and other resources to help you get started with a big day or big year.

## BirdLife International | *birdlife.org*

An international nonprofit for bird conservation. This is a great place to learn and get involved with conservation efforts worldwide.

## Birdability | *birdability.org*

A group that focuses on increasing accessibility in birding. They give guidance and hold events for those with mobility challenges.

## Feminist Bird Club | *feministbirdclub.org*

A group that's dedicated to promoting inclusivity in birding, especially for the LGBTQIA+ community,

BIPOC, and women. There are chapters throughout North America.

## IDENTIFICATION RESOURCES

### Merlin
An app that allows you to identify birds from audio, photos, or a description. You can also keep a list of species you've seen here for personal use.

### Field Guides
Established brands for field guides include Sibley and Peterson.

For young birders, try *The Young Birder's Guide to North America*, by Bill Thompson III, and *Stokes Beginner's Guide to Birds*, by Donald and Lillian Stokes.

## BIRD BOOKS THAT AREN'T FIELD GUIDES

- *Braiding Sweetgrass*, by Robin Wall Kimmerer
- *The Feminist Bird Club's Birding for a Better World*, by Molly Adams and Sydney Golden Anderson
- *The Backyard Bird Chronicles*, by Amy Tan

- *Better Living Through Birding*, by Christian Cooper
- *Slow Birding*, by Joan E. Strassmann
- *Conversation with Birds*, by Priyanka Kumar
- *What It's Like to Be a Bird*, by David Allen Sibley

## BONUS RESOURCE: BIRDING BACKPACKS

A number of libraries now let people borrow birding backpacks that include binoculars, field guides, and other gear needed for a birding day. It's a great way to access this equipment and try it out at no cost.